WITH EVERY FIBER IN ME

PALMWINE PUBLISHING

CHIOMA ROSEMARY ONYEKABA

Copyright © 2024 Chioma Rosemary Onyekaba

All rights reserved. No part of this publication may be reproduced, distributed, or transmitted in any form or by any means, including photocopying, recording, or other electronic or mechanical methods, without the prior written permission of the publisher, except in the case of brief quotations embodied in critical reviews and certain other non-commercial uses permitted by copyright law.

ISBN (Paperback) - 978-1-917267-10-6
ISBN (E-Book)- 978-1-917267-11-3
Published by Nubian Republic on behalf of Palmwine Publishing Nigeria Limited.

Email: info@palmwinepublishing.com
Address- UK: 86-90, Paul Street, London EC2A 4NE
Address-Nigeria: 1A Jos Road Bukuru, Plateau State, Nigeria.
www.palmwinepublishing.com
www.raffiapress.com | www.nuciferaanalysis.com
Cover design: Chioma Rosemary Onyekaba
First Edition: August, 2024

AUTHOR'S LINKTREE:
HTTPS://LINKTR.EE/CHIOMA_ONYEKABA

ABOUT THE AUTHOR

Chioma Rosemary Onyekaba is a trailblazing Nigerian writer, poet, and creative powerhouse whose literary journey began in Jos in 1993. With a foundation in English Language and Literature from Abia State University, Uturu, and a master's degree in Parliamentary Administration from the University of Benin, she has woven her academic insights into a flourishing career that spans multiple creative disciplines.

A versatile artist, Chioma excels as a web designer, photographer, editor, graphic designer, and branding expert. Her dynamic expertise is reflected in her extensive portfolio, with "With Every Fiber in Me" marking her fourteenth published work. Among her other celebrated titles are "Wives Are for Rainy Days, Side Chicks Are for Best Days," "Paradox of Forever," "Wellspring of Emotions," "More Serious Than Tears," "The Secret Diary of an

Obsessed Lover," "Just Before Midnight," "In the Depth of My Thoughts," "My Country, My Pride," "The Rise and Fall of the Shadows of Power," "The Doom That Became My Boom," "The Man with the Midas Touch," "Silent Tears," and "August Lust", all of which explore profound themes with depth and emotional resonance.

Hailing from Eluama in Isuikwuato, Abia State, Chioma is more than just an accomplished author; she is a dedicated entrepreneur and the visionary Managing Director and CEO of Beauty & Brains Foundation (B.B.F.) Printing Press Nig. Ltd, Chioma's Literary Services, Cromstar Studio, BBF Beauty Lounge, and other ventures. Her creativity knows no bounds, as she channels her passion into publishing the prestigious All Times Global Magazine and leading various businesses that showcase her ingenuity.

Chioma Rosemary Onyekaba stands as a wellspring of wisdom and a voice for many, inspiring others to embrace their talents and pursue their dreams with unyielding dedication.

With every fiber in me

Poetry distills the spirit of existence. When life blazes brightly, it leaves behind the tender embers of that radiant journey.

_ Chioma Rosemary Onyekaba

With Every Fiber in Me Chioma Rosemary Onyekaba

Table of Contents

A Bride Unscripted	1
Fractured Mirror	4
The He-Daughter	7
The Awe-Inspiring Creator	12
Love is Law	14
Unbroken	17
The Ember's Edge	20
A Sigh for Nigeria	25

Table of Contents

Love is a Bruised Peach	**28**
Peace Over Pieces	**30**
Clinging to Calmness	**32**
One Life	**34**
Drive Safely on This Road Called Life	**36**
Secret Whispers	**40**
Narcissists	**42**
The Devil's Echo	**43**

Table of Contents

The Heart of Men	**47**
Mushroom that Breaks the Earth	**49**
Whispers of a Shattered Heart	**51**
Queens of Resilience	**54**
Under the Village Moon	**59**
Unseen Depths of Pain	**62**
Whispers of a Silent Warrior	**64**
The Silent Betrayal	**67**

Table of Contents

Echoes of Desire	**68**
Silent Cradle	**71**
Why Seek Validation?	**74**
Rose is Not Just Petals & Scents	**80**
The Return of the Writer's Ink	**83**
Home Memories & Melodies	**86**
I Will One Day Be Free	**89**
If Tomorrow Comes Today	**92**

A Bride Unscripted

Moonlight, a mocking spotlight,
paints the white sheets cold,
A cruel reflection of the veil I
shouldn't lose hold.
Three A.M. techno throbs, a twisted
wedding march,
Taunting the lullabies my head
desperately parch.

Two hundred faces flicker in a
sleepless ballet,
Guests, family, a spectacle I
orchestrated, they say.
The Mehta's grand debut, a Goan
fairytale spun,
My wedding, a masterpiece, before
the unraveling begun.

With every fiber in me by Chioma Rosemary Onyekaba

But escape, not diamonds, dances in my frantic mind,
A bride transformed, from planner to fugitive I find.
This tangled web, a masterpiece of indecision's art,
A chronic flaw that threatens to tear my world apart.

No time for beauty sleep, no time for bridal bliss,
Just the urgent need to untangle this, this wedding's abyss.
For unlike chipped polish, a quick morning fix,
This crisis looms, a happily ever after on the brink.

Fractured Mirror

She is a woman, a mirror cracked and shattered.
When she speaks, her words are echoes in a silent chamber.
When she is slapped, her pain is a silent scream.
When she is loved, it is a fragile glass that can shatter at any moment.

She is a mother, a daughter, a wife, a sister, a friend.
But she is also a woman, a being defined by her gender.

She is expected to be quiet, to be patient, to be submissive.
She is expected to be strong, to be independent, to be successful.
But she is also a woman, a human being with her own desires, her own dreams, her own fears.

With every fiber in me by Chioma Rosemary Onyekaba

She is a woman, a mirror broken into countless pieces.
And yet, she is whole.

She is a woman, a survivor.
She is a woman, a rebel.
She is a woman, a force of nature.

She is a woman, a mirror cracked and shattered.
But she is also a woman, a masterpiece of resilience.

The "He-Daughter"

A chilling tale,
With eerie whispers, fearsome spun,

Beneath the moon's pale, ghostly sheen,
A haunted house, a ghastly scene,
Where specters roam and spirits run,
In moonlit dance, they're not alone.

The creaking floorboards, how they groan,
Invisible hands, a chilling touch,
In every corner, fear does clutch,
A sonnet of dread, a sinister pun.

In mirrors, faces twisted, scorned,
Their mournful wails, a sound forlorn,
The haunting echoes, one by one,
A poem to chill, when day is done.

With every fiber in me by Chioma Rosemary Onyekaba

So hark, dear son, to this dark rhyme,
Where terror dwells in every line,
Let shivers crawl and nightmares won,
For in these words, the scare's begun.

In a village shrouded by twilight's shroud,
Lived a woman, her story profound,
Enigma wrapped her life's every mile,
For she bore no son, just a daughter's smile.

A mystery veiled in whispers and veils,
The townsfolk's superstitions and tales,
Condemned her fate, so unjust and cold,
A woman cursed for what she couldn't hold.

With every fiber in me by Chioma Rosemary Onyekaba

She nurtured dreams, like a garden in bloom,
In her daughter's eyes, dispelling the gloom,
But shadows of doubt, like an endless stream,
Haunted her life, a relentless, cruel theme.

They said her womb was barren, a sign,
Of some unseen sin, an unholy design,
Yet she held her head high,
with grace and pride,
Defying the whispers, she stood by her side.

Her love for her daughter,
unyielding and strong,
Defied the world's judgments,
all the day long,
In this tale of mystery, courage did run,
A mother's devotion, her only son.

With every fiber in me by Chioma Rosemary Onyekaba

For she knew in her heart, a truth so profound,
That love knows no gender, no limits, no bound,
In her daughter's laughter, her life had begun,
And that love was enough, to outshine the sun.

So, let this tale of mystery unfurled,
Speak of a woman, her love for her world,
A son, she had, in her daughter's embrace,
A love so profound, no curse could erase.

The Awe-Inspiring Creator

Who commands the lightning and
directs its path,
Who beholds the hidden treasures in
the vast snow-filled skies?
Who envisioned the sun and sparked
its brilliant flame,
Then veiled its light to grant us the
gentle calm of night?

No one can comprehend!
Incomparable, beyond measure,
You set the stars in the heavens,
And call each one by name.
You are an awe-inspiring God!

All-powerful, unconstrained,
We stand in awe, falling to our knees,
With hearts full of reverence,
You are an awe-inspiring God!

Love is Law

Forget the gavel's heavy thud, the
parchments cold and dry,
Love's law transcends the courtroom,
beneath a boundless sky.

No judge presides in this domain, no
juries cast their vote,
Just hearts entwined, a silent vow, a
love that cannot rote.

This law is writ in gentle touch, in
whispers soft and kind,
In laughter shared, in tears embraced,
a solace for the mind.

It bids us build, not tear apart, to
mend with steady hand,
To see the good in one another, on
shifting, sacred sand.

Love's law demands compassion's touch, forgiveness freely given,
To understand another's soul, a gift from deepest heaven.

It breaks the chains of selfishness, and casts out fear's dark hold,
A symphony of giving hearts, a story yet untold.

So let this law of love resound, in every whispered word,
In selfless deeds, in loyalty, a love that's ever heard.

For though the world may falter, and empires rise and fall,
Love's law endures, a constant flame, that conquers one and all.

Unbroken

They served you shege
You served them food
They showed disdain, treating you with shame,
Yet you served kindness, and never played the same game.

They plucked from your garden, took without care,
You let them cruise, but the scars were always there.

Their laughter echoed, while you quietly bled,
They scorned and danced all reggae and blues with emotions misled.

Your heart heavy with remnants of wounds from the past,
You watched, unable to cry, as time moved so fast.

You were brave, never seeking revenge or spite,
With the same knife they cut you,
they forced you to leak your wounds dry
Yet your resolve stayed upright.

Suddenly they want no eye for an eye, it's a bizarre, comic lie.
They've forgotten the person you were before the strife,
But your strength and grace will define your life.

So before you choose same person again,
Remember how you suffered alone,
healed alone, conquered them all, while they glowed with joy over your pains.

The Ember's Edge

The love she held for him once blazed,
Yet on that night, it dimmed to grey.
A cold ember now, where fire once stayed,
The moment she found his heart astray.

His touch, a ghost, now felt so cold,
As silence wrapped her in its veil.
Days bled into a story untold,
Where every breath was a whispered wail.

Yet, within the hollow of her chest,
A flicker of that love remained,
Stubborn as the sun that won't rest,
In a sky where darkness reigned.

With every fiber in me by Chioma Rosemary Onyekaba

His call came like a distant bell,
A sound that echoed through her night.
A fragile hope within her swelled,
But shadows danced just out of sight.

Could they rebuild what was once strong?
A bridge of trust over betrayal's tide?
Or would her heart, where scars belong,
Be marked by battles fought inside?

She knew, with a certainty so cold,
This wasn't weakness, not a mere façade.
Her love was a tale fiercely told,
A warrior's heart beneath the shard.

But forgiveness is no simple art,
Not bought with roses or spoken charms.
The smile she gave masked a fractured heart,
A wounded soul with open arms.

Her love for him was strength's true face,
Not a naive, foolish thing.
It weathered storms with stoic grace,
But scars were left where pain did sting.

Respect, not love alone, she craved,
A cornerstone on which to build.
For love can fade if not engrained,
In trust and truth, forever sealed.

With every fiber in me by Chioma Rosemary Onyekaba

The choice now lies within his hand,
To cherish love so rare, so deep.
Will he be worthy of her stand,
Or lose the heart he failed to keep?

A Sigh for Nigeria

When people saw the clip of a famished dog
struggling to eat wood in place of bones
They laughed.
I cried.

"Poor dog", you thought.
"Poor nation", I knew.
I wish tears were left to cry,
For already my pot of tears have run dry.

They couldn't wait for death
To serve its deserving members hell,
They served hell to everyone else
And argued first that this was not yet hell.

What is the difference between hell and here?
Nothing but the absence of hell fire and immortals;
For this hell on earth burns not just the flesh,
But everyone with conscience.

They sold pain so cheap
That all the poor may find it easy to buy
And for peace they made it scarce
Tripled the price to the extent that only some elites
could afford that so expensive ride.

With every fiber in me by Chioma Rosemary Onyekaba

They planted division everywhere
United they stood
While watching the poor fall.
Not just fall on muddy grounds,
But a fall that left their tongues as
towels for the feet of their oppressors,
And yet they said
"Bow! Bow you must at my feet"
How do we even bow when our faces
are flat in muddy slumps?
Allow us to please sigh not the type
you won't hear
But a profound sigh that plasters our
pain in your stony hearts forever!

Love is a Bruised Peach

Love is a bruised peach, sweet and yielding at its core, but with a tender imperfection on its skin. It's the ache in your smile after a fight that ends in laughter. It's the phantom limb of an absence, a constant reminder of the warmth that once filled that space.

Love is pain, not because it's meant to hurt, but because it exposes us. We lay bare, hearts on worn sleeves, vulnerable to the gentlest touch and the harshest blow. We risk rejection, disappointment, and the sting of love unreturned.

But love is also the hand that reaches out to cradle the bruised peach, the one that promises to cherish its imperfections alongside its sweetness. The forgiveness whispered after a harsh word, the unspoken understanding that binds two souls together even in the storm.

Love is a bittersweet symphony, a melody that dances between joy and sorrow. It's the tears that fall freely after a shared dream, the knowledge that true connection comes with the risk of heartbreak.

With every fiber in me by Chioma Rosemary Onyekaba

Peace Over Pieces

I love nobody so much
that I'd crumble if they left,
for the echoes of loneliness
have whispered secrets too cruel to forget.
I saw things no eyes should behold,
shadows cast by memories
that slither and bite in the dark.

I cried out to the night,
prayed for sleep to fold me in,
to cradle this restless heart
that knows no refuge in dreams.
And now, this fragile peace,
this threadbare sense of self
I clutch as if it were the sun itself.

For I was stabbed in the heart
a billion times by trust,
each wound a song,
each scar a shield,
and yet, here I stand,
not whole, but not broken—
not finished, but unyielding.
I am the warrior in my own story,
writing my name in the stars
with every breath I refuse to surrender.

With every fiber in me by Chioma Rosemary Onyekaba

Clinging to Calmness

You see this peace I cradle close,
A refuge found in silent night,
Where whispers of despair have flown,
And shadows dim in softest light.

This calm, a gift from battles past,
Where heartache's reign has lost its sway,
No more the chains of sorrow's grasp,
No more the tears that marked my day.

The storm within has now subsided,
The restless waves, now gentle, still,
This quiet joy, my soul's abiding,
A strength that bends to none but will.

I've left behind those ghostly fears,
Those echoes of a troubled mind,
In place of doubts and endless tears,
I've found a peace, no strings to bind.

So here I'll rest, in sweet embrace,
Of calm that soothes, of hope that stays,
I'll cling to this till Jesus' grace,
Calls me to where His love displays..

With every fiber in me by Chioma Rosemary Onyekaba

One Life

Fifty has come, fifty has gone,
But age is just a number, don't be withdrawn.
They say at fifty, you're growing old,
But to die at fifty, you're still young and bold.

Don't let pressure weigh on your heart,
Life's a journey, play your part.
They say a friend of a rich man isn't rich too,
But a friend of a thief becomes one, it's true.

Use your mind, think it through,
Not everything they say is always true.
Enjoy your week, make it bright,
Life's a gift, hold on tight.

With every fiber in me by Chioma Rosemary Onyekaba

Drive Safely on This Road Called Life

On the winding roads of life we tread,
Paths uncharted, both straight and bent,
With dreams as headlights, bright ahead,
And hearts as engines, never spent.

Drive safely on this road called life,
Where speed can thrill but caution saves,
Beware the crossroads of strife,
And cherish every moment it paves.

Each sunrise is a green light's glow,
A chance to journey, to explore,
Yet heed the signs that softly show,
The hazards are waiting to implore.

Beware the fog of doubt and fear,
That clouds the vision and blurs the way,
Let hope be your compass, clear,
To guide you through the darkest day.

The lanes of love and friendship keep,
Close to the shoulder, steady, near,

With every fiber in me by Chioma Rosemary Onyekaba

For in their presence, solace deep,
Finds strength to steer, to persevere.

At times the road may twist and turn,
With potholes deep and bridges frail,
But from each bump, there's much to learn,
Each detour tells a different tale.

Drive safely on this road called life,
For each mile is a story spun,
In moments of joy, in times of strife,
The journey and the destination are one.

With gratitude for every mile,
Embrace the journey, smooth or rough,
For in the end, it's not the style,
But the love you give that's enough.

So grip the wheel with steady hands,
And navigate with heart and mind,
On this vast road that life commands,
May your journey be kind, your spirit find.

Drive safely on this road called life,
In every breath, a chance to thrive,
Through calm and storm, peace and strife,
Embrace the ride, and be truly alive.

With every fiber in me by Chioma Rosemary Onyekaba

Secret Whispers

Just because you shut the door behind the bomb,
Doesn't mean the silence will defuse its roar.
In the quiet hush where shadows calm,
Its ticking heart will still implore.

You sealed the room with trembling hands,
Hoping the echo of the past would fade.
Yet time's relentless, shifting sands
Bear witness to the choices made.

The lock may hold, the frame may brace,
But memories, like shrapnel, fly.
In the stillness, faces trace
The fragments of a hidden sky.

No barrier can block the sound
Of what was set in motion there.
The blast awaits, though doors are bound,
In the echo of despair.

So in the pause between each breath,
When peace seems near, but still unsure,
Remember, silence cannot stifle death—
The bomb's embrace is always pure.

With every fiber in me by Chioma Rosemary Onyekaba

Narcissists

Beneath the gilded glass they stand,
Crafting tales with careful hand,
A world of mirrors, bright and clear,
Where truth is what they wish to hear.

Their voices smooth, like honeyed wine,
Each word a thread in twisted twine,
They weave their lies, a perfect art,
A web to snare the trusting heart.

But in their eyes, no light is seen,
A hollow depth, a vacant sheen,
For in their souls, the truth decays,
A shadowed maze of endless plays.

They wear a mask, so finely made,
A smile that never seems to fade,
Yet underneath, the cracks run deep,
Where silent demons softly creep.

Their love's a blade, so sharp and cold,
A story bought, a heart they sold,
They drink from wells of empty praise,
And dance within their mirrored maze.

With every fiber in me by Chioma Rosemary Onyekaba

But mirrors, too, can turn and bend,
Reflecting lies they can't defend,
And when the glass begins to crack,
The truth they fear comes flooding back.

For in the end, the lies unwind,
No place to hide, no peace to find,
The mirror shatters, shards of pain,
A fractured soul, a hollow name.

So let them spin their tales and boasts,
And raise their glass in hollow toasts,
For truth will find them, soft and slow,
In shadows where the mirrors go.

With every fiber in me by Chioma Rosemary Onyekaba

The Devil's Echo

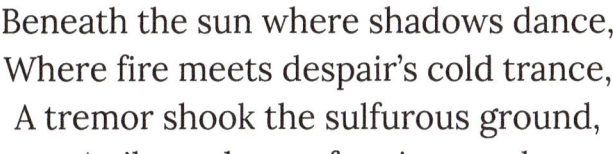

Beneath the sun where shadows dance,
Where fire meets despair's cold trance,
A tremor shook the sulfurous ground,
A silence born of eerie sound.

The plains of Gehenna, steeped in flame,
Paused in the midst of endless shame,
The damned, they faltered, lost in fear,
For something darkened Hell's veneer.

Within the castle, black as night,
Where even demons feared the light,
Lucifer, with eyes aglow,
Felt a disquiet start to grow.

His horns, once proud, now slightly bent,
His thoughts a storm, his mind a vent,
"Azazel!" came the voice of dread,
The air grew still, the shadows spread.

The demon bowed, his bones a quake,
For in his heart, a fear did wake,
"My Lord," he croaked, a hollow sound,

With every fiber in me by Chioma Rosemary Onyekaba

As if the words were tightly bound.

"A change," said Lucifer, pacing slow,
"An imbalance I cannot know,
A shift within the fabric torn,
A whisper of the night reborn."

Azazel trembled, skull aglow,
For he had felt that undertow,
But dared not speak of things unsaid,
Of whispers from the realms of dead.

"They say," he murmured, voice like dust,
"The Devil's name lies in the rust,
They say, My Lord," and here he paused,
A silence deep as death's cold jaws.

"They say... the Devil's breath has stilled,
That Hell itself with dread is filled,
They say," and here his voice did die,
"They say the Devil's meant to die."

With every fiber in me by Chioma Rosemary Onyekaba

A laugh, dark as the void's embrace,
Escaped from Lucifer's twisted face,
"Mortals and their foolish lore,
A dead Devil? What's more?"

Yet in his core, the doubt did creep,
A seed of fear, a pit so deep,
"Send Belial," the order came,
"To find the source of this dark claim."

The shadows shifted, the night grew cold,
As Hell awaited tales untold,
And in the dark where whispers lie,
The Devil's echo asked: "Could I die?"

With every fiber in me by Chioma Rosemary Onyekaba

The Heart of Men

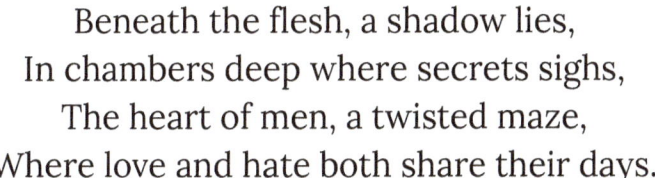

Beneath the flesh, a shadow lies,
In chambers deep where secrets sighs,
The heart of men, a twisted maze,
Where love and hate both share their days.

With silver tongues, they promise gold,
Yet cold as stone, their truths unfold,
A flicker of light, then comes the night,
Deceit and pride their guiding light.

In gentle hands, they hold the flame,
But watch it burn without a name,
No tear, no sorrow marks their way,
For in their hearts, no guilt will stay.

The smiles they wear, a practiced art,
But darkness dwells within their heart,
A place where empathy grows thin,
And only greed and malice win.

Yet hope endures, a fragile thread,
For some, though few, choose love instead,

With every fiber in me by Chioma Rosemary Onyekaba

But still, beware the heart of men,
For once deceived, it wounds again.

So tread with care, and guard your soul,
For in this world, the heart's control,
Can lead to ruin, pain, and woe,
A wicked path where shadows grow.

With every fiber in me by Chioma Rosemary Onyekaba

Mushroom that breaks the earth

Mushroom that breaks the earth without a hoe.
Squirrrel that feasts from the Chlorophora excelsa.
Woman of many parts.
The one who is pushed but not torn.

For you Solitude became a source of strength.
Your scorched soul was lulled by the soothing tone of silence.

You fought and defeated the demons that gnawed at you with the "thunder of patience".

For no reason should you break at any point.
Life is faced by the fearless and you are a true definition of a WARRIOR.

With every fiber in me by Chioma Rosemary Onyekaba

Whispers of a Shattered Heart

Where love once bloomed,
She found a man who wore a mask of light,
But beneath, a storm brewed, silent and doomed,
Leaving her lost in the dark of night.

His words were honey, sweet to taste,
Promising skies that were never true,
But his love, a treacherous waste,
Turned her world from vibrant to blue.

She held on tight, blind in her faith,
Believing his lies, embracing his touch,
But in his arms, she met her wraith,
A lover who never cared too much.

His kisses, once warm, now felt cold,
Each touch a dagger, each word a knife,
In his embrace, she grew old,
Betrayed by the man she called her life.

Yet through the tears, she found her voice,
To rise above the wreckage and pain,
No longer bound by his cruel choice,
She reclaimed her heart, her love, her name.

With every fiber in me by Chioma Rosemary Onyekaba

So here she stands, with scars to show,
A heart that learned to love again,
For though she loved the wrong man so,
She has grown beyond his shadowed reign.

With every fiber in me by Chioma Rosemary Onyekaba

Queens of Resilience

This is for you, the warriors of heart,
Who've stitched your dreams back together with
a thread made of hope,
You, who woke one morning to find your
aspirations
Tucked away in a dusty attic, buried beneath
love's weight.

You married love, embraced commitment with
open arms,
But somewhere along the winding road,
Your own desires slipped through the cracks,
Lost in the shuffle of life's relentless dance.
But listen closely, queens,
Your worth isn't defined by a ring or a name.
The fire that once ignited your passions
Hasn't been extinguished, only dimmed by
circumstance.

The detours you've taken haven't erased the map
Etched in the chambers of your soul,
The one that leads to your personal Everest,
A peak still waiting for your triumphant ascent.

With every fiber in me by Chioma Rosemary Onyekaba

Yes, the heartbreak may sting,
And the sacrifices may weigh heavy on your spirit,
But they've also forged a strength within you,
A resilience as brilliant as a diamond, unbreakable.
Use that strength to rewrite your story,
To redefine success on your terms,
Not bound by society's fleeting expectations,
But by the dreams that still dance in the quiet of your heart.

Rediscover the forgotten melodies,
The songs that once made your spirit soar,
Explore the uncharted territories of your soul,
And chase the opportunities that make you feel alive again.
You are the architect of your destiny,
The author of this next bold chapter.
This isn't the end, darling; it's merely a plot twist,

With every fiber in me by Chioma Rosemary Onyekaba

A chance to rise from the ashes, reborn and magnificent.
Don't let heartbreak hold you captive,
Instead, embrace the journey of healing,
The rediscovery of who you are—
A woman who dares to dream once more.
Find your tribe, those who celebrate your every victory,
Big or small, who hold your hand as you reach for the stars.
You are not alone in this; a legion of women
Have walked this path and now stand beside you, cheering you on.
So unfurl your dreams, let them fly like defiant flags in the wind.
Cast aside society's narrow expectations.
You are a force of nature, a woman reborn,
Trust in your resilience, the unwavering spirit that has brought you this far.

With every fiber in me by Chioma Rosemary Onyekaba

The pages of your story are waiting to be filled,
Not with the echoes of heartbreak,
But with the audacious adventures of a queen
Who dared to reclaim her dreams,
And who conquered her mountain with grace and fire.

With every fiber in me by Chioma Rosemary Onyekaba

Under the Village Moon

In a village where the river hums,
And the night is kissed by the scent of earth,
Two hearts found each other in the quiet hum,
Of a life woven with simple mirth.

By the old baobab, where the elders rest,
They met with eyes that spoke like dawn,
No words needed, just a tender crest,
Of smiles that stretched from dusk till morn.

Her laughter, like the rustle of leaves,
His touch, like the whisper of the breeze,
In the fields where the wildflowers weave,
They sowed their love, with gentle ease.

Their love wasn't gilded, nor wrapped in gold,
No riches did they seek, no fortune did they find,
But in each other's arms, they held the world,
In the simplest things, they intertwined.

He brought her wild honey, sweet and pure,
She made him garlands of the brightest bloom,

With every fiber in me by Chioma Rosemary Onyekaba

Together, they built a love that would endure,
A love that outshone the brightest moon.

In the village square, where stories unfold,
Their love became the tale the old folks tell,
Of how true love isn't bought or sold,
But grows in hearts where honesty dwells.

For in their eyes, the village saw,
That love is more than a fleeting glance,
It's a promise made without a flaw,
A lifelong dance, a timeless trance.

True love, they taught, is not in grand displays,
But in the quiet moments, the everyday,
In the way he held her hand as they walked the maze,
Of life's simple, winding, uncharted ways.

And when the sun set behind the hills,
And the crickets sang their lullaby,

With every fiber in me by Chioma Rosemary Onyekaba

Their love, like the river, stills,
But never fades, never says goodbye.

For in the village where the river hums,
And the night is kissed by the scent of earth,
Their love lives on in the quiet drum,
Of two hearts that knew true love's worth.

With every fiber in me by Chioma Rosemary Onyekaba

Unseen Depths of Pain

There's a depth to pain no words can trace,
A silent place, no smile can face.
It lingers deep, beneath the skin,
Where only those who've lived it, begin.

It's in the night, when voices sleep,
In endless shadows, it runs deep.
A hollow ache, a whispered scream,
That steals away the brightest dream.

No touch can reach, no hand can mend,
This wound that hides, this endless bend.
For pain is more than tear-streaked eyes,
It's the weight behind each masked disguise.

Yet, if you feel it—truly know,
The scars it leaves, the way it grows—
You'll find within, a quiet grace,
A strength born from that darkest place.

For only those who've touched this fire,
Can understand the soul's desire
To rise again, despite the fall,
And stand, though pain may still enthrall.

With every fiber in me by Chioma Rosemary Onyekaba

A depth no one can touch but you,
A place where only truth breaks through.
Pain, unseen by every gaze,
But in your heart, it finds its blaze.

This poem captures the unique, personal experience of pain, reflecting its deep emotional layers. Let me know if you'd like any adjustments!

With every fiber in me by Chioma Rosemary Onyekaba

Whispers of a Silent Warrior

I don't fight wars you'll ever see,
No banners raised, no loud decree.
But in the quiet of my soul,
Battles rage that make me whole.

I won't recount them from afar,
They're not the kind that leave a scar.
But if you wish to know the truth,
Draw closer, I'll share the proof.

For in my eyes, a storm resides,
In my silence, strength abides.
Come near, and listen if you dare,
To stories few would ever share.

Not every fight is in the fray,
Some wars are fought in hearts each day.
So step into this quiet space,
And you'll see battles time can't erase.

But I won't shout or call you near,
For only those with hearts sincere
Will feel the pull, the quiet plea:
If you seek truth, then come to me.

With every fiber in me by Chioma Rosemary Onyekaba

A depth no one can touch but you,
A place where only truth breaks through.
Pain, unseen by every gaze,
But in your heart, it finds its blaze.

With every fiber in me by Chioma Rosemary Onyekaba

The Silent Betrayal

I gave you the sun, but stood in the rain,
Poured my light, yet lived in pain.
Every smile I wore was stitched with thread,
Of wishes unsaid, of words left dead.

I danced to the rhythm of your every need,
In a garden of sorrow, I planted each seed.
Yet the blooms that grew were never mine,
Tangled in thorns, lost in time.

In shadows, I lingered, craving your grace,
But in the mirror, I lost my own face.
Each gift, each favor, a slice of my soul,
Leaving me hollow, far from whole.

Now I see, the cost is clear—
The hands I fed left scars so near.
People pleasing, a quiet ache,
Where hearts like mine are bound to break.

With every fiber in me by Chioma Rosemary Onyekaba

Echoes of Desire

Groans echo like a wounded beast,
A cry of longing, a plea for release,
From bruises that throb deep in the bone,
Aching with the weight of flesh alone.
Caught in tangled vines that cling,
Bound in places where desires sting,
A pulse beats wild, but the path is lost,
Searching for the solace passion costs.

Moans rise up in breaths of fire,
A hymn to hunger, a chant of desire,
The body's music, primal and raw,
Sung in the language of flesh and awe.
With every touch, the pulse climbs higher,
Seeking the place where sparks inspire,
Velvet whispers and tender heat,
The merging of heartbeats, incomplete.

Both groans and moans carve out a space,
Where yearning dwells and time gives chase,
To moments spent in rapture's thrall,
As bodies fall and rise, then fall.

With every fiber in me by Chioma Rosemary Onyekaba

In groans, there's struggle, in moans, release,
A dance that seeks a deeper peace,
Two voices that tremble in the dark,
Leaving traces, like an ember's spark.

With every fiber in me by Chioma Rosemary Onyekaba

Silent Cradle

Unheard cries linger in the quiet air,
Little hearts paused before they beat,
Dreams unformed drift where angels stare,
Tiny hands closed, never reaching to meet.

In a world unchosen, they softly fade,
Gentle spirits taken before they could stay,
No lullabies to soothe or tears to evade,
Their only cradle—heaven's soft sway.

Little souls whispered in the breath of time,
Echoes of love that never got to grow,
Silent footsteps that never learned to climb,
Stars dimmed before they had a chance to glow.

Who will grieve for the life not begun,
For a heartbeat hushed in the secret night?
Their stories were written, but then undone,
Erased from a page where darkness took flight.

But somewhere beyond the touch of pain,
Where light and peace eternally embrace,

With every fiber in me by Chioma Rosemary Onyekaba

They gather in clusters like drops of rain,
Filling the sky with a quiet grace.

Aborted babies, gentle and free,
Your silent existence was still meant to be.
Not forgotten, though brief was your stay,
In our hearts, you live—never swept away.

With every fiber in me by Chioma Rosemary Onyekaba

Why Seek Validation?

She stands, questioning the need to be seen,
Why should she crave what others deem?
Her truth burns bright, a steady flame,
Yet still, she wonders why she seeks a name.

She's built her dreams on a quiet hill,
With hands that shape and a heart of will,
But finds herself searching for wandering eyes,
That measures her worth or let it slide by.

Is it weakness that makes her yearn,
For the glow that others' praises burn?
Or is it simply the way of the soul,
To need a voice that says she's whole?

She asks for no gold, no crowns to wear,
But for someone to see, to know, to care.
A nod, a smile, a word to embrace,
To soften the edge of the world's harsh face.

Validation—a brief touch,
She knows it shouldn't be the thief,
Of peace she seeks, yet it means much,
A mirror that holds her doubts in clutch.

With every fiber in me by Chioma Rosemary Onyekaba

Perhaps it's more than pride's own plea,
Perhaps it's hope that she longs to be,
To know that her voice, though faint, is heard,
That she can leave a mark with every word.

So she steps into the light, faces the crowd,
Not for applause, not to feel proud.
But to touch a heart, to find her place,
To know she is seen in this vast, vast space.

With every fiber in me by Chioma Rosemary Onyekaba

Why Seek Validation?

She stands, questioning the need to be seen,
Why should she crave what others deem?
Her truth burns bright, a steady flame,
Yet still, she wonders why she seeks a name.

She's built her dreams on a quiet hill,
With hands that shape and a heart of will,
But finds herself searching for wandering eyes,
That measures her worth or let it slide by.

Is it weakness that makes her yearn,
For the glow that others' praises burn?
Or is it simply the way of the soul,
To need a voice that says she's whole?

She asks for no gold, no crowns to wear,
But for someone to see, to know, to care.
A nod, a smile, a word to embrace,
To soften the edge of the world's harsh face.

Validation—a brief touch,
She knows it shouldn't be the thief,
Of peace she seeks, yet it means much,
A mirror that holds her doubts in clutch.

With every fiber in me by Chioma Rosemary Onyekaba

Perhaps it's more than pride's own plea,
Perhaps it's hope that she longs to be,
To know that her voice, though faint, is heard,
That she can leave a mark with every word.

So she steps into the light, faces the crowd,
Not for applause, not to feel proud.
But to touch a heart, to find her place,
To know she is seen in this vast, vast space.

With every fiber in me by Chioma Rosemary Onyekaba

Rose is not just Petals & Scents

She refuses to play the victim's part,
Not just a rose but a woman with heart.
Born equal, with a mind that's sharp,
Not defined by curves or a softened arc.

Why should she be sacrificed to settle debts,
Or be dirtied by duties she never met?
Not for her father's burden, her mother's whims,
Nor to keep a brother's path from growing dim.

She will not trade dignity for a grade,
Or use her body as the price to be paid.
Her mind is her might, her voice is her blade,
Her worth is not in the games others played.

So speak to her face, for there's a mouth,
A voice that carries both strength and doubt.
Do not lull her with taunts or feigned favor,
She will not cower to a false savior.

No more will she bend to a weakened lie,
That calls her less, with no right to defy.
She sees the servitude in being kept,
Knows there's more to life than silent steps.

With every fiber in me by Chioma Rosemary Onyekaba

For if she is compared to a cat's soft fur,
Let them remember her claws that stir.
A rose is not just petals and scent,
But thorns and roots—her spirit's lament.

No longer will excuses bind her fate,
She chooses courage, refuses to wait.
Her worth is beyond what others see,
A right to air, a right to be free.

Stand tall, woman—let sobriety show,
Not in the rose but in all you know.
For if your value is measured in bloom,
Let your voice fill every room.

Scream 'til someone hears, speak 'til they care,
Demand respect—claim your share.
For you are more than a fragile name,
You are fire, strength, and unending flame.

With every fiber in me by Chioma Rosemary Onyekaba

The Return of the Writer's Ink

The writer's ink comes home at last,
No longer lost in shadows cast.
From distant shores where muses play,
It flows with purpose, ready to stay.

Once hidden in doubt and despair,
Each drop now whispers, secrets to share.
It gathered dust on forgotten pages,
Yearning for warmth through the passing ages.

With every stroke, a tale takes flight,
Echoes of dreams stirring in the night.
Restless spirits breathe life anew,
In words that speak both bold and true.

The ink returns with stories to tell,
Of laughter and heartache, of heaven and hell.
From parchment skies to paper seas,
It dances and flows, moving with ease.

Each bottle holds a universe spun,
Of battles fought and victories won.
It glimmers with truth, shines with grace,
Reclaiming the voice that time can't erase.

With every fiber in me by Chioma Rosemary Onyekaba

So gather your pages, ignite the flame,
Let ink reclaim its rightful name.
For in its depths, the world expands,
With every drop, the magic stands.

The return of the writer's ink is near,
A symphony sung in whispers clear.
It paints the silence in vibrant hues,
A canvas is alive with the poet's muse.

As twilight falls and shadows recede,
The ink flows freely, fulfilling its creed.
Capturing moments, both laughter and pain,
Weaving through life like a gentle rain.

So welcome the ink, let it flow like a stream,
A river of thought, a well of dreams.
For in its return, the writer finds grace,
An endless journey, an eternal embrace.

With every fiber in me by Chioma Rosemary Onyekaba

Home Memories & Melodies

As dawn breaks, shadows begin to play,
Melodies from home drift softly in.
Laughter echoes in the morning light,
Filling the hallways, warm and bright.

The kettle hums a familiar tune,
Sunshine chases away the remnants of night.
A symphony of scents wafts through the air,
Warm bread rising, love laid bare.

Children's voices weave dreams anew,
Binding together under skies of blue.
Each sound a memory, rich and deep,
Moments we cherish and hold and keep.

The leaves rustle gently in the evening breeze,
Nature's orchestra plays with effortless ease.
Crickets join in, their serenade sweet,
A lullaby drifting, soft and complete.

As dusk falls, stars begin to shine,
Fireflies flicker, weaving magic divine.
In every corner, a song takes flight,
Melodies of home, pure and bright.

With every fiber in me by Chioma Rosemary Onyekaba

When distance calls and the heart feels alone,
These familiar tunes bring comfort back home.
Every note carries the weight of our ties,
Guiding the wanderer under starlit skies.

Let the music of home flow and grow,
In the heart's quiet spaces, let it glow.
With each cherished memory, may it remind,
Home is a melody forever entwined.

With every fiber in me by Chioma Rosemary Onyekaba

I Will One Day Be Free

You can chain me to your will,
Strike me down with your iron chill,
Twist your tongue with lies and skill,
Mock my dreams, bend them still.

But my spirit won't be sold,
You cannot shackle what is bold.
You cannot steal the love I hold,
Nor dim the light I keep untold.

For I will one day rise and be free,
Free to walk the path meant for me,
Free to shape the world I see,
Free to choose who I wish to be.

You can seize what's in my hand,
Bury my voice beneath your command,
Turn my days to dust and sand,
Rally your power across the land.

But you cannot erase my song,
Or bind the place where I belong.
You cannot silence what's been strong,
The right to fight what's always wrong.

With every fiber in me by Chioma Rosemary Onyekaba

For I will one day rise and be free,
Free to breathe, to laugh, to be,
Free to sail across every sea,
Free to live unbound, fully me.

I resist the weight you bring,
I deny your broken ring.
The wind will shift, the dawn will sing,
And I will be free, I will take wing.

With every fiber in me by Chioma Rosemary Onyekaba

If Tomorrow Comes Today

If tomorrow comes today, what shall we say?
Shall we whisper to the dawn that we've lost our way?
Will we clutch at dreams that arrived too soon,
Or dance in the glow of a midday moon?

The sun, unbidden, rises ahead,
Spilling light on the paths we thought we'd tread.
Promises once sealed for another time,
Now unravel, like poems without rhyme.

If tomorrow comes today, will we know its face?
Or stumble, startled, in this unplanned embrace?
Will we cherish the moments we couldn't delay,
Or mourn the sunsets that drifted away?

The future folds into the present's breath,
Each heartbeat trembling, escaping death.
Plans are like leaves in an autumn breeze,
Shifting, swirling, with effortless ease.

With every fiber in me by Chioma Rosemary Onyekaba

If tomorrow comes today, would we dare to be bold?
To chase forgotten dreams, to let stories unfold?
Or would we fear what the fates have spun,
And retreat from a journey we've just begun?

Let us welcome the hours, whether near or far,
Trace the lines of fate like scars on a star.
For if tomorrow comes today, come what may,
We shall rise with the dawn, unafraid to stay.

www.ingramcontent.com/pod-product-compliance
Lightning Source LLC
Chambersburg PA
CBHW072049160426

43197CB00014B/2697